Sometimes People Fight

Even When They Love Each Other

Written and illustrated by
Dagmar Geisler

Translated by
Andrea Jones Berasaluce

Sky Pony Press
New York

Sky Pony Press books may be purchased in bulk at special discounts for sales promotion, corporate gifts, fund-raising, or educational purposes. Special editions can also be created to specifications. For details, contact the Special Sales Department, Sky Pony Press, 307 West 36th Street, 11th Floor, New York, NY 10018 or info@skyhorsepublishing.com.
Sky Pony® is a registered trademark of Skyhorse Publishing, Inc.®, a Delaware corporation.

Visit our website at www.skyponypress.com.
10 9 8 7 6 5 4 3 2 1
Manufactured in China, June 2019
This product conforms to CPSIA 2008

Library of Congress Cataloging-in-Publication Data is available on file.

Cover provided by Loewe Verlag GmbH
Cover illustration by Dagmar Geisler

Print ISBN: 978-1-5107-4654-1
Ebook ISBN: 978-1-5107-4665-7

Sometimes We Fight

Not long ago, picture books served to teach children appropriate behavior. They presented the stereotypes of the then "ideal family": strict father, silent mother, good child. Fighting? Never! And if so, then nobody should know about it!

Sometimes We Fight—Even When We Love Each Other is light-years away from that ideal. Dagmar Geisler's book about living together breathes new life, with a free spirit, into this subject. The mother walks around in socks. The parents roll dice to see who gets to make plans for their weekend. And the child is always in the middle of it all.

The best part: we still learn something. How disputes arise. That it doesn't always work without arguments. How to end quarrels. How to reconcile afterward. Misunderstandings and conflicting interests are normal. The first we can clarify, the second requires creative handling. This is the case with children as well as with parents and—smiling, we discover—also with dogs and cats.

The third issue is the most sensitive: when the cause and the event are unrelated. It is just trouble brewing from before. Mom admits to being "stressed at work," Dad says he has "a lot on his plate." This book is a valuable foundation for joint discovery. It does not hide that quarrels are also scary. They can be a thing of nightmares. Not even stuffed animals can offer comfort. The morning must be endured along with a quarrel at kindergarten. Then, finally, flowers and apologies.

Relieved—and wiser—the child and parents set the book aside. And it rings true. Even the dog and cat learn the lesson: "Arguing is part of life, but getting along is much nicer."

Dr. Martina Steinkühler,
Professor of Religious Pedagogy

Do you sometimes argue with others?

Almost everyone argues at some point.

The Müllers sometimes argue about nothing.

The Meiers often squabble over soccer.

Olga and Ben bicker every time they want to go on vacation.

The Quapps sometimes have a spat over TV programs.

Bella and Fido fight over treats.

Even people who like each
other disagree sometimes.

Ernst and Annemarie sometimes argue about
what's better: thrillers or love stories.

We never fight!

My Dad ⟶

⟵ My Mom

Only my parents never argue.

No, that's nonsense, of course.

These two are not angels, after all.

However, they're usually very nice and funny.

There are days, though, when I feel something in the air.

I can see it in Mom's eyebrows . . .

. . . or in the way Dad is silent.

Drip drop . . .

. . . and in
Dad's mouth.

I notice it
when Mom
just sits
there . . .

CRASH

Sometimes it's just a misunderstanding.

Like the day Dad thought Mom threw away his favorite old T-shirt. It was just in the wash.

Sometimes they have very different opinions.
Just like the day Mom felt like taking a trip,
and Dad absolutely wanted to visit Grandma.
They fought for a little bit, but then
found a solution together.

But once it was really bad.

At breakfast, I noticed something was wrong.

As we drove to the zoo, Mom was at the wheel and Dad made a strange face and looked out the window the whole time. They didn't talk, and in the rearview mirror, I noticed the biggest crease I've ever seen in Mom's forehead.

She always has that when she gets angry.

At first, I thought they might be annoyed with me. But when we later walked through the zoo, they were both very, very nice to me.

They barely spoke to each other, though. (Only when they thought I couldn't hear them hissing at each other.)

I had to go to bed shortly after we got home, but I couldn't sleep. I heard how they argued loudly. They even slammed doors. (They don't ever let me slam doors.) Then it sounded like someone was crying.

At breakfast the next morning, Mom had very sad eyes and Dad was not there at all. I didn't dare ask if he had already gone to work.

At kindergarten, I was in a terribly bad mood and I was suddenly very mad at Leon. I yelled at him. Just because he asked if we should finish building our castle. Of course, his feelings were hurt, and that really bothered me. Leon is my best friend and we really wanted to finish building our castle.

Mom was still acting funny in the afternoon. She didn't even scold me when I turned on the television without asking.

But then Dad came home. He had a big bouquet of flowers with him. He gave it to Mom and said: "I'm sorry that we argued and I was so stubborn. But I was in a bad mood because I have so much on my plate."

And Mom said, "I'm sorry, too, I was unfair because I'm stressed at work right now."

So you weren't mad at each other?

No. Maybe . . .

A little bit.

I was grumpy because you barely talked to me.

And I was grumpy because you forgot to go shopping. After work, I really wanted to have some of my favorite cheese.

So cheesy!

"I was afraid that you no longer loved each other and wanted a divorce."

"Oh dear, it was that bad?" Mom and Dad asked, quite worried.

And I nodded, because it was really that bad.

And I wanted them to promise me they would never fight again.

But that's not how it works, they said. Fights happen in even the strongest and closest of families. That's part of it, even if you don't like it.

The important thing is that you make up again. And that you can then talk about why you were fighting.

Sometimes quarrels arise through misunderstandings. This can be clarified.

Or people argue because they have different opinions. They can find a compromise.

And sometimes you begin to argue about something that has nothing to do with the other person. If that happens, you can ask for forgiveness.

Adults fight sometimes, and so do children.

SORRY!